Betty Junor

Fun Funky Knits

BARRON'S

First North American edition published in 2012
by Barron's Educational Series, Inc.

Copyright © The Five Mile Press Pty Ltd, 2012
Illustrations by: Jack Vanzet
Photography by: Greg Els Photography
Images on pages 5, 6, 10, 11, 28, 34, 48, courtesy of Shutterstock

All inquiries should be addressed to:
Barron's Educational Series, Inc.
250 Wireless Blvd.
Hauppauge, New York 11788
www.barronseduc.com

ISBN: 978-1-4380-0174-6
Library of Congress Control No.: 2012932175

Printed in China
9 8 7 6 5 4 3 2 1

Contents

Introduction

Knitting is fun—and it's not hard to do! In a few simple steps, you can learn the basic skills you need to create your own funky knits, such as scarves, hats, headbands, and lots more. All the knits in this book are easy and quick—and most of them only use one ball of yarn and one pair of US 10.5 (6.5 mm) needles!

The thickness of the yarn that you use on these needles will create different styles of knits. For example, thicker yarn will make a tight knit, while thin yarn will make a loose knit. At the beginning of each project, you'll be told what size of yarn to use to get the look in the photo.

Once you have mastered the classic knit stitch on these US 10.5 (6.5 mm) needles, a section at the end of the book offers you some other projects that you can try, using different-sized needles and other types of yarns.

The final chapter shows you how to jazz up your creations with buttons, beads, chains, cords, pompoms, and embroidery—you'll be amazed at how easy it is to make all these gorgeous things. Have fun experimenting with materials and decorations. Craft stores are a paradise of amazing wools and yarns, buttons, beads and ribbons, and will inspire you to create incredible projects that you never thought you could.

So pick up your needles, grab some funky yarn, and start creating your own simple knits!

Knitting basics

This is where the fun begins! In this chapter, you'll find everything you need to know about the equipment and basic techniques for making the fab creations in this book.

Gather your supplies
Needles and yarn

The first thing you need to think about when you're going to knit something is the thickness of the yarn and the size of the needles you will use. This book makes it simple. Most of the projects use one set of US 10.5 (6.5 mm) needles and **What you'll need** on each page tells you the thickness, weight and type of yarn that has been used to create the funky knits in the photographs. However, there are all sorts of needles and yarns you can buy. Here's a quick overview of how it all works.

Which needles?

The first thing you should know is that different countries use different measurements for their needle sizes, so a size 10.5 needle in the United States is called a 6.5 mm needle in Australia and Europe and a size 3 needle in Britain. Standard knitting needles range from US 0 (2 mm) to US 35 (19 mm). This measurement relates to how thick the needles are. The smaller the needle, the smaller the stitches will be. The thicker the needle, the bigger the stitches will be.

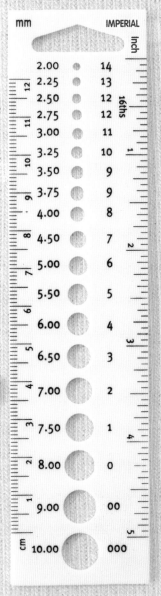

mm	IMPERIAL inch
2.00	14
2.25	13
2.50	12
2.75	12
3.00	11
3.25	10
3.50	9
3.75	9
4.00	8
4.50	7
5.00	6
5.50	5
6.00	4
6.50	3
7.00	2
7.50	1
8.00	0
9.00	00
cm 10.00	000

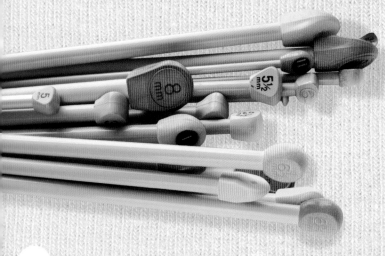

What yarn?

The size of yarn refers to the thickness of the thread. This is called the "ply" of the yarn. The most common yarns are from fingering- to bulky-ply, with fingering being the thinnest and bulky the thickest. Thin wool will make your stitches small, but your knit looser, while thick wool will make your stitches bigger and your knit tighter.

Yarn and needles combo

So, if you use thick needles and thick yarn, you will have big, thick stitches.

If you use thick needles and thin yarn, your stitches will be loose.

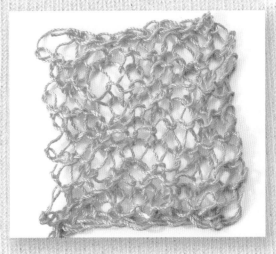

If you use thin needles and thick yarn, your stitches will be tight.

If you use thin needles and thin yarn, you will have small stitches.

Different types of yarn

There are many different types of yarn—both man-made and natural—and each creates a different effect. "Natural" yarns are those that come from animals or plants, such as wool, cashmere, alpaca, silk, bamboo, or cotton. Man-made fibers include acrylic, viscose, polyester, and nylon.

Some yarns are 100% natural and others are a mixture of both. The band on a ball of yarn will always tell you exactly what it is made of, so be sure to check.

Choosing the right yarn

The type of yarn you choose will be determined mostly by the project that you are planning. Plain, smooth yarn will create a classic knit and is easiest to use when you are learning to knit because you can see what you are doing clearly. As you get more confident, try to experiment with other yarns you can find—some have sparkles in them, some are fluffy or bumpy, while others change from thick to thin in the one thread!

While it is most important to think about the size and texture of the yarn you want to use, it's also good to note what it's made from and the washing instructions. If you are making something that you will need to wash frequently, and don't like hand washing, look for machine-washable wool or perhaps an acrylic yarn. Also, some people are allergic to pure wool and might need to choose an acrylic yarn so that it doesn't prickle and make them itchy.

Ball bands

When you buy a ball of yarn, it is wrapped around with a label called a "band" (see below). This tells you about the yarn—what it is made of, how you should wash it, how much the ball weighs, and what size needles are normally used to knit it.

In this book, we're not going to worry too much about all this, because we are mostly

using US 10.5 (6.5 mm) needles with all our yarns. Sometimes, your projects may be a slightly different size than ours if you use a slightly different yarn—but it won't matter, as long as you use a yarn that is reasonably similar.

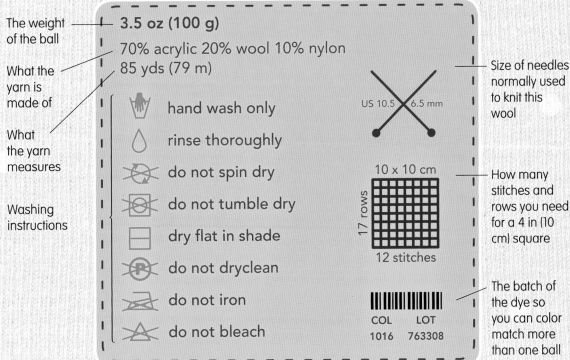

The weight of the ball

3.5 oz (100 g)

What the yarn is made of

70% acrylic 20% wool 10% nylon

What the yarn measures

85 yds (79 m)

Washing instructions

hand wash only

rinse thoroughly

do not spin dry

do not tumble dry

dry flat in shade

do not dryclean

do not iron

do not bleach

US 10.5   6.5 mm

Size of needles normally used to knit this wool

10 x 10 cm

17 rows

12 stitches

How many stitches and rows you need for a 4 in (10 cm) square

COL   LOT
1016   763308

The batch of the dye so you can color match more than one ball

Other materials

Needles and yarn are the main materials used in this book to create the knits, but there are also a few other necessary things.

Things you will need:

• A **big needle** with a large eye and blunt end (also called a tapestry needle or knitter's needle), so that you can stitch your fabulous knitted garment together. These needles are bigger than ordinary sewing needles.

• **Pins** to hold the edges of your knitting together when you are sewing seams

• A pair of **scissors** to cut wool, cotton, or ribbon

• **Embroidery needle** for embroidering

• **Sewing thread and needle** to sew on beads and buttons

• **Tape measure** or ruler to measure the length of your knitting

• **Embroidery thread** for embroidering

Things you might want:

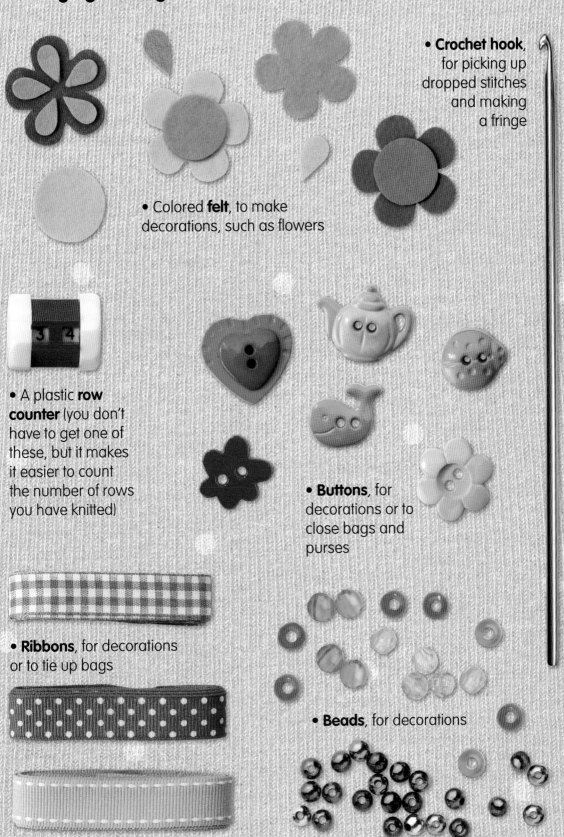

- **Crochet hook**, for picking up dropped stitches and making a fringe

- Colored **felt**, to make decorations, such as flowers

- A plastic **row counter** (you don't have to get one of these, but it makes it easier to count the number of rows you have knitted)

- **Buttons**, for decorations or to close bags and purses

- **Ribbons**, for decorations or to tie up bags

- **Beads**, for decorations

Getting started

Now that you have your needles and yarn, let's begin! The first thing you have to do is attach the yarn to the knitting needle. You do that with a loop called a slipknot.

Making a slipknot

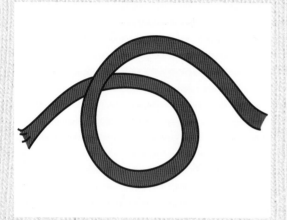

1. Take the end of your ball of yarn and make a loop a short distance from the tail.

2. Pull the yarn through the loop to make another loop.

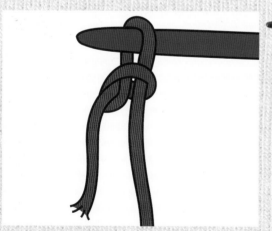

3. Push one of your needles through the new loop and pull the ends of the yarn until the loop is firm on the needle, but still able to slide.

Tip
Sometimes a pattern will tell you to leave a tail of yarn when making your slipknot. This is so you can use the tail to sew up the seams of your knitted piece at the end, rather than having to attach a new piece of yarn.

Congratulations—you have made a slipknot, which is your first stitch!

Casting on

These instructions, and those on the following pages, are for right-handers. If you're a lefty, hold the pictures up to a mirror and you'll see instructions just for you! You only need one needle for this type of casting on, which is called "single cast on" or "e-loop cast on."

1. Hold the needle with the first stitch on it in your right hand.

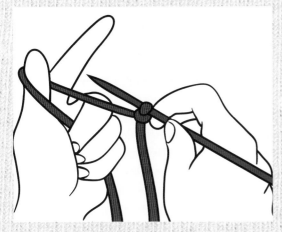

2. Wrap the yarn around your left thumb.

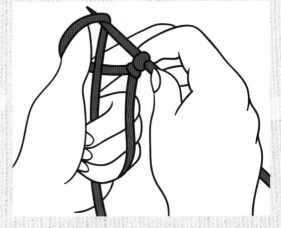

3. Insert the needle under and through the loop on your thumb, then slide your thumb out.

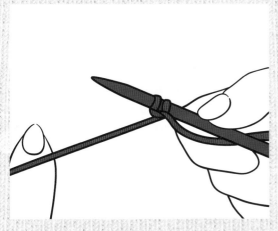

4. Pull gently on the yarn to tighten the stitch on the needle—now you have two stitches!

5. Repeat steps 2 to 4 until you have the number of stitches that you want.

You have now cast on and are ready to knit your first row!

Basic knit stitch

Now that you have cast on, it's time to learn how to knit! This is how to do basic knit stitch, the stitch that is used in this book. To make things easier for you to follow, we've used two different colored needles, but yours will both be the same color.

To begin, hold the needle with the stitches on it (purple) in your left hand, between your thumb and index finger. Hold the empty needle (pink) in your right hand.

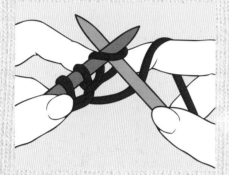

1. Push the point of the pink needle through the middle of the first stitch on the purple needle.

"In through the front door ..."

2. With your right hand, take the yarn around the back of the pink needle, then bring it between the needles, from the back to the front.

"Once around the back ..."

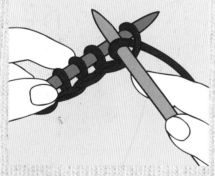

3. Holding the yarn tight, carefully slide the purple needle up to the tip of the pink needle until you can bring the tip of the pink needle through the stitch on the purple needle. Pull the loop through with your pink needle.

"Out through the window ..."

4. You have now made a new stitch on the pink needle. Slide the pink needle along to the tip of the purple needle and slip the new stitch off the purple needle, moving it fully to the pink needle. You've now done a complete stitch!

"And off jumps Jack."

5. Repeat Steps 1 to 4 until you have knitted all the stitches from the purple needle to the pink needle.

6. When you have finished this first row, swap the needles around so the full needle (now the pink needle) is in your left hand and the empty needle (now the purple needle) is in your right hand. Now you are ready to knit the next row—but this time, you will be transferring the stitches from the pink needle to the purple needle.

Tip
Here's a little traditional rhyme to help you remember the order of the steps:

In through the front door,
Once around the back,
Out through the window,
And off jumps Jack.

When you work every row in knit stitch like this, it is called "garter stitch" and that is the stitch used for all the projects in this book.

Tip
If you're having trouble getting the hang of knit stitch and you have access to a computer, look for a beginner's tutorial on the Internet. There are plenty to choose from and you might find it easier to follow moving hands than diagrams.

Starting a new ball or a different color

When your yarn runs out or you want to start a different color, you should always join the ends of the balls at the beginning of a row. This looks much neater than having a join in the middle of your knitting. Cut your old yarn about 4 in (10 cm) from the needle. Tie your new yarn onto the old yarn with a knot, as close as possible to the needle.

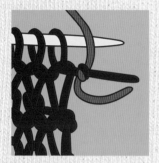

Now you can keep knitting with the new yarn. When you've finished knitting, remember to sew in the ends (see page 19), by weaving them along the edge of your knitting.

(see page 19)

Tip
To check if you have enough yarn to finish a row, lay the yarn loosely across your knitting from side to side. You need enough to go at least from side to side and back again. If you think you won't have enough, start another ball. It's better than running out just a few stitches from the end of a row—and you can always use the leftover yarn to sew up seams.

Counting the rows

As you knit each row, your knitting will gradually get longer and longer. Sometimes a pattern will tell you to knit for a certain length, say 4 in (10 cm), and you can measure this with a tape measure. Other times, the pattern will tell you to knit a certain number of rows. You can use a row counter on the end of your needle and turn it every time you finish a row, or you can make a mark on a piece of paper at the end of each row. But if you forget, then you have to learn how to count the rows on your knitted piece.

Look carefully at the piece of garter stitch below. It is made up of bumpy ridged rows with little "valleys" in between. (If you are looking at your own knitting, you can see the valleys more clearly if you stretch the ridges apart a little.) Each of those bumpy ridges equals 2 rows, so if you count the ridges and multiply that number by 2, you will know how many rows you have knitted. The very first cast-on row does not count as a row.

Ridges

Valleys

What to do if you drop a stitch

When you accidentally slip a stitch off your needle, this is called a "dropped stitch." You can't leave it, because it will unravel and leave a big, ladder-like hole in your work. Luckily, a dropped stitch is easy to fix. Here's how.

1. If you're not already at the spot where you've dropped the stitch, pop a safety pin through the dropped stitch, then knit across the row until you reach the safety pin.

2. Carefully remove the safety pin. The dropped stitch should be in between your needles. The loose strand of yarn should be in front of the dropped stitch.

3. Push your right needle through the dropped stitch from the back to the front, then under the strand of yarn that has been left behind.

4. Using the left needle, lift the dropped stitch over the strand of yarn and off the needle. This forms a new stitch on the right-hand needle.

5. Push your left-hand needle through the new stitch, and transfer the stitch back onto the left-hand needle. Check that the stitch isn't twisted the wrong way—there should be a little "bump" below the stitch. If it is twisted the wrong way, use your other needle to turn it so it sits the right way.

Binding off

Now that you have mastered the knitting part, it's time to learn what to do at the end so that your knitting won't unravel when you take it off the needles. When your work has reached the length that you need, here is what to do to finish it off.

Start by holding the needle with the stitches in your left hand and the empty needle in your right hand.

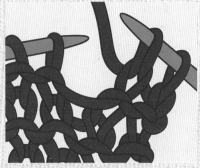

1. Knit two stitches, just like you were knitting an ordinary row.

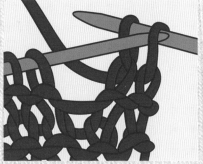

2. Insert the tip of the left-hand needle into the first stitch that you knitted.

3. Lift the first stitch over the top of the second stitch and let it drop off the tip of the needle. You have just bound off one stitch!

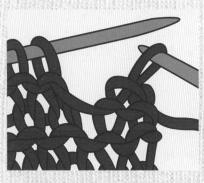

4. Now you are left with only one stitch on the right-hand needle.

5. Knit another stitch from the left-hand needle in the usual way and repeat Steps 2 to 4 to bind off a second stitch.

Repeat this process until you only have one stitch left on the right-hand needle.

6. Slip the needle from the last stitch and pull the stitch open so that it becomes a big loop. Cut the yarn from the ball, thread the end through the loop, and pull it up tightly to fasten it off.

There you go!
A finished funky knit.

Finishing

Weaving in the ends

Once you have your finished piece, you need to tie up all the loose ends! This is called "weaving in the ends" and it's important because it leaves your work looking neat and also makes doubly sure that your knitting will not unravel at any point.

1. Thread the end of the yarn into your large needle with the blunt end.

2. Using the needle, thread the loose end through the edge of your knitting for about 5 rows.

3. Cut the end close to your knitted piece.

4. Repeat for each loose end of yarn.

Sewing up seams

Most knitted garments will need to have the edges, or seams, sewn up to complete them. The method used in this book is called an "overcast stitch." We've used a different colored yarn to show how to sew the seam, but you should use the same color as your knitting yarn, so that the stitches will be almost invisible!

1. Start by holding your two knitted edges together, with their right sides facing each other, that is, the wrong sides are on the outside. You can pin the edges to make it easier to keep them straight, but you don't have to.

2. Thread some yarn onto your large needle and make a knot in the end.

3. Sew the knot inside the seam so that you can't see it from the outside.

4. Use the needle to sew over and over the edge of the knitting (see opposite) until you get to the end of the seam.

5. Pull the yarn back through the edge of the knitting to fasten it. Cut off the end.

6. This seam will be on the inside of your project. Turn the knitting right-side out to see how neat it looks on the outside.

Sewing on buttons

Not everything you knit will need a button, but lots of things do—sometimes for fastening an opening, or just because buttons are fun! Sewing on a button is one of the most useful things you will ever learn to do, so here's how.

1. Thread your needle and make a knot in the other end. Normally, you would use a sewing needle and cotton, but if you are sewing a button onto a knitted project, you will probably use your large needle and the same yarn that you knitted with. (Make sure that the needle will fit through the holes in the button.)

2. Bring the needle from the back of the knitting to the front, at the spot where you want the button to be.

3. Thread the needle through the first hole on the button, from the back to the front, then take it back down into the second hole, from the front to the back.

4. Now take it back through the knitting to the back again. Pull the thread through until the button is sitting securely on the knitted fabric.

5. Now thread your needle up through the button and back down again once or twice more.

6. Finally, take the needle to the back and weave it through several stitches to make sure the thread is secure. Snip off the end.

The Projects

Now that you have learned the basics, it's time to put your cool new skills into action!

Wide scarf

Scarves are great for putting your new knitting skills into action. They are long and straight and you don't have to count the rows, just stop knitting when the scarf is long enough. Add beads and fringes—get creative!

Measurements

Our scarf measures 5 in (13 cm) wide and 33 in (85 cm) long, but make yours any length you like!

What you'll need

• One 110 yd (100 m) ball of bulky yarn

• One pair of US 10.5 (6.5 mm) needles

• Large needle, for sewing in the ends

• Beads (optional)

Here's how

1. Cast on 16 stitches.

2. Work rows in knit stitch until the scarf is as long as you want. A good length to stop is about 33 in (85 cm).

3. Bind off.

4. Use your large needle to weave in the ends of the yarn (see page 19).

Finishing

1. The scarf in the picture has 8 fringes on each end. If you want to add fringing, check out the easy instructions on page 70.

2. One way to add some extra sparkle to your scarf is to thread some beads on the ends (see page 71). This is simple to do and looks great. If you want to add beads, choose beads with a large enough hole to thread the yarn through—remember, the yarn is quite thick.

Tip
The fringe on your scarf can be any color or yarn that you like. If you want the fringe to match the scarf however, make sure you leave enough yarn when you bind off to use as fringing.

Thin scarf

This thin scarf is twice as quick to knit as the wide scarf because you only have to work with 7 stitches on each row, instead of 16 stitches. So choose your favorite color and get knitting.

Measurements

Our scarf measures 2 in (5 cm) wide and 41 in (105 cm) long, but make yours any length you like!

What you'll need

• One 1.75 oz (50 g) ball of bulky yarn

• One pair of US 10.5 (6.5 mm) needles

• Large needle, for gathering the ends and attaching pompoms

Here's how

1. Cast on 7 stitches, leaving a short tail about 4 in (10 cm) long.

2. Work rows in knit stitch until you have used up all of the yarn.

3. Bind off, leaving a short tail of about 4 in (10 cm) before cutting the yarn.

Tip
If you want a longer scarf, you will need two balls of yarn!

Finishing

1. Use the "tails" that you left at the beginning and end of your knitting to gather the ends of your scarf.

2. To gather an end, hold the opposite corner to the one with the tail on it and pull the tail with your other hand. The edge will gather together.

3. Pull the tail as tight as you like, then tie it off and weave in the extra yarn (see page 19).

4. Use the ties from the pompoms to sew them to your new scarf!

Tip
If you want a pompom on each end of your scarf, make them first so you can use the rest of your yarn for the scarf. Check out page 72 for pompom instructions.

Frilly scarf

This scarf is actually wider than the "wide scarf," but is gathered at each end, making it curl up. So it curls properly, the knit stitch needs to be looser than the other two scarves, which means using thinner yarn.

Measurements

Our scarf measures 5½ in (14 cm) wide and 39 in (100 cm) long, but yours can be any length you like!

What you'll need

• One 1.75 oz (50 g) ball of bulky yarn

• One pair of US 10.5 (6.5 mm) needles

• Large needle, for gathering the ends and attaching pompoms

Here's how

1. Leaving about 6 in (15 cm) of yarn at the start, cast on 20 stitches.

2. Work rows in knit stitch until you have used up all of the yarn. The scarf in the picture measures 5½ in (14 cm) wide and 39 in (100 cm) long.

3. Bind off, leaving a tail of about 6 in (15 cm) before cutting the yarn.

Tip
If you want a longer scarf, you will need two balls of yarn!

Finishing

1. Use the "tails" that you left at the beginning and end of your knitting to gather the ends of your scarf.

2. To gather an end, hold the opposite corner to the one with the tail on it and pull the tail with your other hand. The edge will gather together.

3. Pull the tail as tight as you like, then tie it off and weave in the extra yarn (see page 19).

4. Use the ties from the pompoms to sew them to your new frilly scarf!

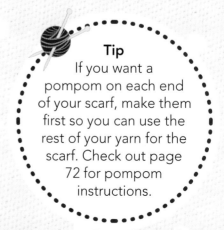

Tip
If you want a pompom on each end of your scarf, make them first so you can use the rest of your yarn for the scarf. Check out page 72 for pompom instructions.

Thin headband

Follow these simple steps to create a headband that is perfect for you. They are so easy to make, why stop at one? Leave your headband plain, or decorate it with buttons or a knitted flower.

Measurements

These headbands are about 3 in (7 cm) wide and as long as they need to be to fit around your head.

What you'll need

• One 1.75 oz (50 g) ball of DK (double knitting) yarn

• One pair of US 10.5 (6.5 mm) needles

• Large needle, for sewing ends together

• Decorative buttons (optional)

• Knitted flower (optional—see page 74)

Here's how

1. Cast on 10 stitches.

2. Work rows in knit stitch until the band fits around your head.

3. Bind off.

Finishing

1. Fold your headband in half so that the short ends match up.

2. Thread your large needle with the same colored yarn as your knitting.

3. Sew the two short ends together (see page 19).

4. Thread the yarn back through the knitting so the end is neatly hidden. Cut off any extra yarn.

5. Now use your needle and yarn to sew on some decorative buttons or a knitted flower. To make these knitted flowers, check out the instructions on page 74.

Wide headband

The secret to the glamorous finish on these headbands is a ring sewn into the seam. You can use any ring that measures approximately 1 in (2.5 cm) across—even the ring from a keyring!

Measurements

These headbands are 3½ in (9 cm) wide and as long as they need to be to fit around your head.

What you'll need

- One 1.75 oz (50 g) ball of Aran weight yarn
- One pair of US 10.5 (6.5 mm) needles
- 1 in (2.5 cm) in diameter metal, plastic, or wooden ring
- Large needle, for sewing the ring in place
- Pins
- Small jewel with holes, or a button or bead (optional)

Here's how

1. Cast on 14 stitches.

2. Work rows in knit stitch until the band fits around your head.

3. Bind off.

Finishing

1. Place one of the short edges of your headband over half of the ring.

2. Fold the edge under the ring. You can pin it to hold it in place if you like.

3. Thread your large needle and sew the edge in place with running stitch (see page 78).

4. Repeat on the other side.

Tip
For extra glamour, sew a jewel, a button, or a bead in the hole.

Hats

Hats not only keep your head warm in winter, but they look cool and save you from bad hair days! Experiment with rolling up the brim, or adding decorations on the bottom or the top.

Measurements

These hats are about 9 in (23 cm) from top to bottom (before the brim is folded up) and will fit a head that measures about 21 in (54 cm) around.

What you'll need

• One 1.75 oz (50 g) ball of chunky pure wool or acrylic mix yarn

OR

• Two 1.75 oz (50 g) balls of DK weight or Aran weight yarn

• One pair of US 10.5 (6.5 mm) needles

• Large needle, for sewing seam

• Decorative buttons, optional

Here's how

1. Leaving about 16 in (40 cm) of yarn at the start, cast on 30 stitches.

2. Work rows in knit stitch until your piece measures 20 in (50 cm).

3. Bind off, leaving about 8 in (20 cm) of yarn to gather the top of the hat.

Finishing

1. Thread the longer tail of yarn onto your large needle. Sew the shorter (cast-on/bind-off) edges of your knitting together to make a tube shape, using an overcast stitch (see page 19).

2. Turn the tube right-side out when you've finished sewing the seam.

3. Thread the other tail of yarn onto your needle and sew in running stitch (see page 78) around one open edge of the tube.

4. Pull the thread firmly to gather the edges and close the top of the hat.

5. Turn up the brim and sew on some decorative buttons, flowers, or beads.

Tip

To make a pompom for your hat follow the instructions on page 72. Use the tie-off threads of the pompom to attach it firmly to the top of the hat. Tie all the ends together and weave them through the knitting on the inside, so they don't show.

Belt

Knitted belts are a great way to put your new skills to use because they are quick to make and can be adapted to fit any size waist. If you want a wider belt than this, simply cast on more stitches.

Measurements

This belt is about 3 in (7 cm) wide and as long as it needs to be to fit around your waist.

What you'll need

• One 1.75 oz (50 g) ball of chunky pure wool or acrylic mix yarn

OR

• One 2.6 oz (75 g) ball of chunky, quick-knit yarn

• One pair of US 10.5 (6.5 mm) needles

• One wooden, metal or plastic ring

• Large needle, for sewing on the ring

• A button

Here's how

1. Leaving a tail of yarn about 8 in (20 cm), cast on 9 stitches.

2. Work rows in knit stitch until your piece is long enough to wrap around your waist or hips, plus a little extra to fold back over and attach.

3. Bind off, leaving a tail of about 8 in (20 cm) before cutting the yarn.

Finishing

1. Wrap one end of your belt through the ring and use the tail of yarn to sew the end in place on the inside.

2. Put the belt around your waist. Push the other end of the belt through the ring and pull it until the belt fits snugly. Sew a button to attach the end to the belt. With the remaining yarn tail make a loop to fit over the button. See pages 66 to 69 for some easy ideas for making loops.

Tip

There are many other ways that you can fasten the ends of your belt together. Here are some easy ones:

• Simply knit your belt a bit longer and tie the ends in a knot.

• Sew Velcro onto the belt opening.

• Pin it together with a big safety pin.

• Sew on a belt buckle—you can buy these from a craft store or take one off a belt you don't use anymore.

• Sew on a big, decorative button.

Bag

Impress your friends with your brilliant bag collection! Make this easy pattern in chunky yarn to go with jeans or try a sparkly yarn and glam it up with jewel-like buttons and beads for parties.

Measurements

Our bag measures 8 in (20 cm) wide and 5½ in (14 cm) high.

What you'll need

• One 3.5 oz (100 g) ball of chunky, quick-knit yarn

• One pair of US 10.5 (6.5 mm) needles

• Large needle, for sewing seam

• Pins

• Two medium buttons

Here's how

BAG

1. Cast on 20 stitches.

2. Work rows in knit stitch until your piece measures about 14 in (35 cm).

3. Bind off.

STRAP

1. Cast on 3 stitches.

2. Work rows in knit stitch until your work measures about 24 in (60 cm).

3. Bind off, leaving 36 in (90 cm) of yarn to attach strap and make loops.

Finishing

1. Place the bag piece with the right side facing up. Fold up the bottom edge until it measures 5½ in (14 cm) from the bottom fold (see diagram 1).

2. Fit one end of the strap between the back and front edges of the bag on one side, so the end of the strap is on the fold line at the bottom (see diagram 2).

3. Pin the strap in place for 5½ in (14 cm) along the back and front edges. Pin the other end of the strap to the other side of the bag.

4. Sew the strap down the front side edge, across the bottom and up the back side edge on both sides, so the strap forms a loop across the top (see diagram 3). The bit of seam that you don't sew at the top will form a flap.

5. Turn the bag right-side out and fold over the flap.

6. Sew buttons on the front of the bag and attach button loops—see pages 66 to 69.

1

2

3

Leg warmers

You don't have to be a dancer to enjoy wearing leg warmers—they look fantastic over leggings. Make them in a plain color or maybe in wild stripes. You can also make a slightly smaller pair for your arms.

Measurements

Measure around your heel and ankle to find how much stretch you need to fit over the widest part of your foot. These will stretch to 11 in (28 cm) so you can pull them over your foot. If your heel and ankle measure more than 11 in (28 cm), you will need to add some more stitches—25 stitches makes 11 in (28 cm), so you would need approximately one more stitch for every extra ⅜ in (1 cm).

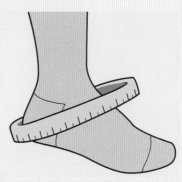

What you'll need

• One 1.75 oz (50 g) ball of wool/alpaca blend yarn (Aran weight)

OR

• Two 1.75 oz (50 g) balls of self-striping 100% wool (Aran weight)
• One pair of US 10.5 (6.5 mm) needles
• Large needle, for sewing seam
• Pins
• Decorative buttons

Helpful hint
If you want them tighter at the top, thread some elastic thread through the inside of the top row, pull it up as tight as you like and tie it off securely.

Here's how

1. Loosely cast on 25 stitches on US 10.5 (6.5 mm) needles. (You need to cast on loosely so that the edge will stretch over your foot.)

2. Work about 77 rows in knit stitch or about 11½ in (29 cm).

3. Bind off loosely.

4. Knit another piece the same as the first.

Tip
You could also make these warmers for your arms. Cast on 22 stitches and knit in the same way as the leg warmers—but maybe a bit shorter.

Finishing

1. Fold each piece in half, so the right sides are facing each other and the side edges are matching. Pin the edges together into a tube.

2. Thread your large needle with yarn and sew a seam along the edges to join them together, using an overcast stitch (page 19). Weave any ends in along the seam so they don't show.

3. Turn the leg warmer right-side out so the seam is on the inside.

4. Decorate with buttons or beads.

Hot water bottle cover

How cute is this—an owl that doubles as a snuggly hot water bottle cover! He'll make you smile every time you pop into your lovely warm bed. Safety eyes are available from craft stores, but you could also use a couple of big buttons.

Measurements

The finished cover measures about 9 in (23 cm) wide and 10 in (26 cm) long.

What you'll need

- Two 2.6 oz (75 g) balls of chunky, quick-knit yarn
- One 1.75 oz (50 g) ball of DK weight yarn in a contrasting color, for eyes
- One pair of US 10.5 (6.5 mm) needles
- Large needle, for sewing seam
- Cut two triangles of felt, one slightly larger than the other.
- Two x 1 in (3 cm) pieces of Velcro tape
- Pins
- Sewing cotton and needle

BODY

Here's how

1. Leaving an 18 in (45 cm) tail of yarn at the beginning, cast on 26 stitches on US 10.5 (6.5 mm) needles, using chunky yarn.

2. Work 117 rows in knit stitch.

3. Bind off, leaving a tail of yarn at the end.

Finishing

1. Fold the body piece in half across the middle, so the right sides are facing each other and the side edges match on each side. Pin the edges together.

2. Thread your large needle with the yarn tail on each side and sew the edges together, using an overcast stitch (see page 19).

3. Turn the body right-side out so the seams are on the inside. You now have a small bag.

4. Using sewing cotton and needle, attach a small strip of Velcro tape to the top edge of the bag at each side of the bottle neck.

FACE

Here's how

1. Using DK weight yarn and US 10.5 (6.5 mm) needles, loosely cast on 30 stitches.

2. Work 5 rows in knit stitch.

3. Bind off, leaving enough yarn to thread through the bound-off edge.

4. Using your large needle, thread the yarn tail through the bound-off edge, pull firmly to gather and fasten off. This will be the center of the eye.

5. Sew up the seam on the short edges. Repeat steps 1 to 5 to make the other eye.

Finishing

1. Push the safety eyes through the center of the knitted eyes and secure them at the back.

2. For the beak, put the small felt triangle on top of the larger one. Position the top edge of the beak under the eyes.

3. Using running stitch (see page 78), sew around the outside of the eyes to fix them in place and attach the beak in place at the same time.

Fingerless gloves

These are perfect for those chilly days when your hands are cold but you still need to use your fingers. Knit them in funky colors or stripes and decorate them with buttons, beads, or felt flowers.

Measurements

These gloves measure 7 in (18 cm) long and about 8 in (20 cm) in diameter. Measure around the widest part of your hand. For every 3/8 in (1 cm) more than 8 in (20 cm) that your hand measures, add an extra stitch when you cast on. For every 3/8 in (1 cm) less around your hand, cast on one stitch fewer.

What you'll need

• One 1.75 oz (50 g) ball of two-toned alpaca/merino bouclé-style Aran weight yarn

OR

• One 1.75 oz (50 g) ball of bright, textured, bulky acrylic yarn
• One pair of US 10.5 (6.5 mm) needles
• Large needle, for sewing seam
• Pins
• Decorative buttons or beads

Here's how

1. Loosely cast on 17 stitches on US 10.5 (6.5 mm) needles. (You need to cast on loosely so that the edge will stretch over your hand.)

2. Work about 40 rows in knit stitch or until piece measures about 7 in (18 cm).

3. Bind off loosely, leaving a tail of yarn for sewing the seam.

4. Make a second piece the same as the first.

Finishing

1. Fold the glove pieces in half, so the right sides are facing each other and the side edges match. Pin the edges together to make a tube.

2. Thread your large needle with the yarn tail and sew the edges to join them together, using an overcast stitch (see page 19).

3. Turn the glove right-side out so the seam is on the inside.

4. Fold the wrist edge of each glove down into a cuff and decorate with buttons or beads to hold the cuff in place.

Wrap skirt

How cool would it be to knit your own skirt? This little wrap skirt can be adapted to fit any size waist and looks gorgeous with a ribbon belt. You could also add a fringe around the bottom if you were feeling really wild.

Measurements

This skirt measures about 13 in (33 cm) from the waist to the hem.

What you'll need

• Two 3.5 oz (100 g) balls of Aran weight acrylic yarn

• One pair of US 10.5 (6.5 mm) needles

• Large needle, for attaching belt loops

• Enough 1½ in (40 mm) wide ribbon, to tie around your waist

• 1 in (3 cm) piece of Velcro tape

• Buttons

• Sewing cotton and needle

Here's how

SKIRT

1. Cast on 40 stitches on US 10.5 (6.5 mm) needles.

2. Work in knit stitch until the skirt reaches around your hips, plus enough overlap to close the gap in the opening.

3. Bind off.

BELT LOOPS

Following the finger knitting instructions on page 67, make enough 2 in (5 cm) long loops to be able to attach one every 10th row. We used 18 loops, but the exact number will depend on how wide your skirt is. When you're making the loops, remember to leave enough yarn at each end to sew the loops to the skirt.

Finishing

1. Attach the belt loop chains to one long edge (the top) of the skirt, placing them every 10th row or so.

2. Thread wide ribbon through the belt loops and tie in a bow to make a belt.

3. Using sewing cotton and a needle, sew the Velcro strip under the edge of the front flap and sew the matching strip to the other edge.

4. Sew buttons to the front of your skirt for decoration.

Mini me
To make a skirt for a doll, cast on 10 stitches to make a 3 in (8 cm) wide skirt. Knit as long as you need to wrap around your doll's waist.

Large cushion cover

Big, soft, cushions make fun accessories. Knit a couple to toss on your bed or on the floor to lounge on while you're watching TV or playing on the computer. Decorate them with big decorative buttons, felt shapes, or flowers.

Measurements

This cover will fit a 16 in (40 cm) cushion.

What you'll need

- Two 3.5 oz (100 g) balls of 12-ply yarn
- One pair of US 10.5 (6.5 mm) needles
- Large needle, for sewing seams
- Pins
- Decorative buttons
- Knitted flower, to decorate (see page 74)
- 16 in (40 cm) cushion insert (see page 77)

Here's how

1. Cast on 50 stitches on US 10.5 (6.5 mm) needles.

2. Work in knit stitch until piece measures about 35½ in (90 cm).

3. Bind off.

Tip
Instead of tucking the flap inside the cover, you could leave it on the outside. To keep it closed, sew two or three chain loops onto the edge (see pages 66–69) and sew on two or three decorative buttons to match the loops.

Finishing

1. With right sides facing each other, fold up the bottom edge toward the center until the side edges measure about 16 in (40 cm).

2. Pin the edges together, then thread your large needle with yarn and sew up each side, using an overcast stitch (page 19).

3. Turn the cover right-side out so that the seams are on the inside. The bit of knitting that is left extending now forms the flap of the cover, like an envelope.

4. Sew a knitted flower or some decorative buttons onto the cover, if you like, taking care not to stitch through both layers or your cushion won't fit inside!

5. Pop the cushion insert into your cover, tuck in the flap (like tucking in an envelope) and you're done.

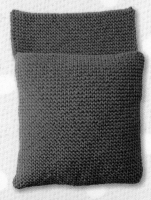

Fluffy pink cushion

This little cushion is unimaginably soft and cuddly. It is knitted by combining two yarns and knitting them together as though they were just one. Take care when you are knitting that you always put your needle through both strands of yarn.

Measurements

The finished cushion is 9½ in (24 cm) square.

What you'll need

- Two 1.75 oz (50 g) balls of DK weight yarn
- Two 1.75 oz (50 g) balls (or about 131 yds/120 m) of eyelash novelty yarn or mohair
- One pair of US 10.5 (6.5 mm) needles
- Large needle, for sewing seams
- Pins
- Three large buttons
- One 9½ in (24 cm) cushion insert (see page 77)

Here's how

1. Using US 10.5 (6.5 mm) needles and one strand of DK weight yarn and one strand of eyelash yarn together, cast on 30 stitches.

2. Work in knit stitch until your piece measures about 24 in (60 cm).

3. Bind off.

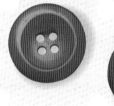

Finishing

1. With right sides facing each other, fold up the bottom edge toward the center until the side edges will cover your cushion.

2. Pin the edges together, then thread your large needle with DK weight yarn and sew up each side, using an overcast stitch (see page 19).

3. Turn the cover right-side out so that the seams are on the inside. The bit of knitting that is left extending now forms the flap of the cover, like an envelope.

4. Put your cushion insert into the cover, fold over the flap and use a pin to mark where the buttons should go.

5. Sew the buttons below the flap (see page 20).

6. Using the DK weight yarn only, make three finger chain loops (see page 67) to fit around the buttons.

7. Sew the ends of the loops firmly to the underside of the flap and secure them around the buttons.

Comfy bed socks

Keep your tootsies warm and cozy in a pair of these knitted socks. Wear them around the house, or wear them to bed on a chilly winter's night.

Measurements

Measure around your heel and ankle to find how much stretch you need to fit over the widest part of your foot. These will stretch to 11 in (28 cm) around your ankle and heel so you can pull them over your foot. If your heel and ankle measure more than 11 in (28 cm), you will need to add more stitches—25 stitches makes 11 in (28 cm), so you would need about one more stitch for every extra 3/8 in (1 cm).

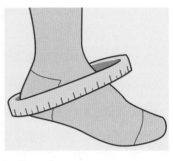

What you'll need

- One or two 1.75 oz (50 g) balls of chunky yarn
- One pair of US 10.5 (6.5 mm) needles
- Large needle, for sewing seams
- Pins
- Narrow ribbon
- Small decorative beads (optional)

Here's how

1. Leaving a tail of yarn for sewing up the toe, loosely cast on 25 stitches, using US 10.5 (6.5 mm) needles. (You need to cast on loosely, so the edge will stretch over your foot.)

2. Work in knit stitch until your sock is as long as you want it to be.

3. Bind off, leaving a tail of yarn for sewing up the center back seam.

4. Make another piece the same size.

Finishing

1. Fold the sock pieces in half, so the right sides face each other and the side edges match. Pin the long edges together.

2. Thread your large needle with the yarn tail and sew the edges together using an overcast stitch (page 19). Position the seam so that it runs down the middle, not the side.

3. Pin the short edges together and stitch this seam to close the toe.

4. Turn the sock right-side out so the seams are on the inside.

5. Thread a ribbon through the knitted top and decorate the ends with a few small beads.

Rug

Knitting squares is easy—and if you knit a lot of squares, you can make this super rug! Choose a few of your favorite colors or maybe make it in the colors of your local team. You could also make a matching cushion.

Measurements

Each DK weight square measures about 5 in (12.5 cm) square. The size of the completed rug will depend on how many squares you decide to knit. As a guide, one 1.75 oz (50 g) ball of DK weight yarn should make four squares.

What you'll need

• 1.75 oz (50 g) balls of DK weight yarn in a number of colors

• One pair of US 10.5 (6.5 mm) needles

• Large needle, for sewing seams

• Pins

Here's how

1. Leaving an 8 in (20 cm) tail of yarn, cast on 22 stitches, using US 10.5 (6.5 mm) needles.

2. Work about 37 rows in knit stitch, or until your piece is a perfect square.

3. Bind off, leaving an 8 in (20 cm) tail of yarn.

4. Make all your other squares in the same way—our rug has 64 squares, but you can knit as many squares as you need for the size of rug you would like.

Tip
For a firmer rug, use 12-ply wool with the same instructions.

Finishing

1. Arrange your squares in rows of equal number. Move the squares around so that the colors are mixed up and nicely distributed.

As you are laying out your squares, vary the direction of the knitted rows so that each alternate square runs in the opposite direction to its neighbors. This will stop your rug from getting too stretchy.

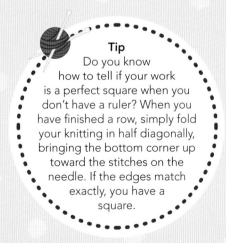

Tip
Do you know how to tell if your work is a perfect square when you don't have a ruler? When you have finished a row, simply fold your knitting in half diagonally, bringing the bottom corner up toward the stitches on the needle. If the edges match exactly, you have a square.

Tip
If you've got lots of bits of yarn leftover, you could make a fringe around the edge of your rug—see page 70.

2. Pick up the first two squares and pin them together along one edge. Try to make sure that the edges match exactly—you can stretch them just a little if you really need to!

3. Using a tail of yarn from one of the squares, sew them together, using an overcast stitch (see page 19). When you get to the end of the seam, take a couple of firm stitches, then weave the tail back through the seam (see page 19) and trim it off.

4. Pin the next square in the row in place and sew it. Sew all the squares in each row together like this.

5. Now sew the rows together, one after another, trying as much as possible to make sure that the seams on each row match each other. You probably won't be able to use yarn tails for sewing these seams, so just use leftover yarn.

6. When you have finished sewing, make sure that all the tails are woven in and trimmed.

Guess what? Your rug is done!

Projects on different needles

Using different yarns with bigger and smaller needles means that you can create a chunky, thick knit for a warm wrap or a tight knit for a purse or bag to keep your treasures safe.

Wrap with flower

Perfect for keeping your shoulders warm in chilly weather, this simple wrap is held together at the front by a button attached to the knitted flower. For extra warmth and softness, choose pure wool or a wool/alpaca mix.

Measurements

This wrap is 10 in (25 cm) wide and about 27 in (70 cm) long using 7 oz (200 g) of yarn. You will need more yarn if you want to make it larger.

What you'll need

- 7 oz (200 g) of super chunky yarn
- One pair of US 13 (9 mm) needles
- DK weight yarn for the knitted flower
- One pair of US 6 (4 mm) needles for the knitted flower
- One small button
- One decorative button (optional)

Here's how

WRAP

1. Cast on 26 stitches on US 13 (9 mm) needles.

2. Work in knit stitch until piece measures about 27 in (70 cm) or the desired length.

3. Bind off.

FLOWER

1. Leaving a tail of about 6 in (15 cm), cast on 30 stitches on US 6 (4 mm) needles.

2. Work in knit stitch for 5 rows.

3. Bind off, leaving a tail of 6 in (15 cm).

Tip
You could use a brooch to hold your wrap together, or make your own (see page 75)

Finishing

1. To make the flower, roll your knitting into a spiral like a rose, and use the tails of yarn to sew across the bottom edge so that it stays in shape.

2. Sew a small button to the bottom of the flower, where it attaches to the wrap. Push the small button through a hole in the "valley" of your knitting, near the top corner of your wrap. Push it through the corner of the wrap underneath to hold both edges together. You could also just pin it with a safety pin.

Drawstring bag

Drawstring bags are ideal for keeping things safe, as you can pull the top closed tightly. Knit them in bright colors or maybe stripes and add decorations to suit your mood, from beads to colorful flowers and embroidery.

Measurements

About 6 in (16 cm) wide and 7 in (18 cm) long.

What you'll need

• One 1.75 oz (50 g) ball of DK weight yarn
• One pair of US 9 (5.5 mm) needles
• Narrow ribbon, for drawstring
• Decorative button or beads (optional)
• Large needle, for sewing seams
• Pins

Here's how

BAG

1. Leaving a tail of yarn, cast on 26 stitches on US 9 (5.5 mm) needles.

2. Work in knit stitch until your piece measures about 14 in (35 cm). Knit an uneven number of rows. This is so that the ribbon threads through the same rows of knitting at the front and the back.

3. Bind off, leaving a tail of yarn.

> **Tip**
> You can use bulky yarn and the same needles if you want a firmer bag.

STRAP

1. Leaving a tail of yarn, cast on 2 stitches, using US 9 (5.5 mm) needles.

2. Work rows in knit stitch until your strap is as long as you want it.

3. Bind off, leaving a tail of yarn.

Finishing

1. Fold the bag piece in half across the middle, so the right sides are facing each other and the side edges match on each side. Pin the edges together.

2. Thread your large needle with the yarn tail on each side and sew the edges to join them together, using an overcast stitch (see page 19).

3. Turn the bag right-side out so the seams are on the inside.

4. Use the tails of yarn on the end of the strap to attach the strap to the bag on each side.

5. Thread narrow ribbon evenly through the knitting around the top edge to make a drawstring.

6. Decorate the bag with a pretty button, or thread beads onto the ends of the ribbon drawstring before knotting the ends together.

Purses

A girl can't have too many purses! They're so easy to knit, you could make one to match every outfit and make them for your friends as well. This combination of yarn and needles gives a firm knitted fabric to hold all your treasures.

Measurements

About 4½ in (11 cm) wide and 4 in (10 cm) high.

What you'll need

- One 1.75 oz (50 g) ball of bulky wool or acrylic
- One pair of US 6 (4 mm) needles
- Buttons
- Large needle, for sewing seams
- Pins

Here's how

1. Leaving a tail of yarn, cast on 22 stitches on US 6 (4 mm) needles.

2. Work in knit stitch until your piece measures about 9 in (23 cm).

3. Bind off, leaving a tail of yarn.

Finishing

1. With right sides facing each other, fold up the bottom edge toward the center until the side edges form a little purse with a flap extending above them, like an envelope.

2. Pin the edges together, then thread your large needle with yarn and sew up each side, using an overcast stitch (see page 19).

3. Turn the purse right-side out so that the seams are on the inside.

4. Fold the flap over and sew a wool or chain loop (see pages 66–69) to the underside of the flap.

5. Sew a button to the front of the purse to match the flap.

6. Sew on smaller decorative buttons too, if you like, so the purse looks like a cute face.

Purse with strap

Adding a strap to your purse means you can slip it over your wrist, or sling it over your shoulder. You can also jazz up the ends of the straps with beads. These purses are the perfect size for a mobile phone or an iPod.

Measurements
About 4½ in (11 cm) wide and 4 in (10 cm) high.

What you'll need
• One 1.75 oz (50 g) ball of bulky yarn
• One pair of US 6 (4 mm) needles
• Large needle, for sewing seams
• Pins
• A button
• Sewing cotton and needle, for sewing strap
• Small beads (optional)

Here's how

PURSE

1. Leaving a tail of yarn, cast on 22 stitches on US 6 (4 mm) needles.

2. Work in knit stitch until your piece measures about 9 in (23 cm).

3. Bind off, leaving a tail of yarn.

Tip
For an extra pretty touch, thread small beads onto the strap before you attach it to the purse.

Finishing

1. With right sides facing each other, fold the bottom edge toward the center to form a little purse with a flap extending above, like an envelope.

2. Pin the edges together. Thread your large needle with yarn and sew up each side using an overcast stitch (see page 19).

3. Turn the purse right-side out so that the seams are on the inside.

4. Fold the flap over and sew a loop or chain (see page 66) to the underside of the flap.

5. Sew a button to the front of the purse to hook the loop onto.

STRAP
Following the instructions on pages 66–69, make a long finger chain, braid, or knitted cord for the strap. It needs to be long enough to stretch along one side of the purse, form a loop as long as you want at the top, then stretch back down the other side of the purse to the bottom. Using a sewing needle and cotton, sew the ends of the strap in place along the side edges of the bag.

Tip
You could also use ribbon for the strap of your purse, instead of a chain.

Sunglasses case

Keep your sunglasses safe and scratch-free in their own little knitted pouch. Use a bright, funky color so it's always easy to find in your bag. You could also knit one of these as a special gift for someone who wears ordinary glasses.

Measurements

This case measures about 3 in (7 cm) wide and 6 in (15 cm) long.

What you'll need

• One 1.75 oz (50 g) ball of bulky wool
• One pair of US 6 (4 mm) needles
• Large needle, for sewing seam
• Pins
• One medium button or bead

Here's how

1. Cast on 14 stitches on US 6 (4 mm) needles.

2. Work rows in knit stitch until your piece measures enough to cover your glasses, about 12½ in (32 cm), plus about 2 in (5 cm) extra, for a flap.

3. Bind off.

Finishing

1. With right sides facing each other, fold up the bottom edge toward the center until the side edges form the glasses case, with a 2 in (5 cm) flap extending above, like an envelope.

2. Pin the edges together, then thread your large needle with yarn and sew up each side, using an overcast stitch (see page 19).

3. Turn the case right-side out so that the seams are on the inside.

4. Fold the flap over and sew a loop (see pages 66–69) to the underside of the flap.

5. Sew a button to the front of the case to hook the loop on to.

Tip
Instead of the button, you can also thread a bead onto a length of yarn that is twice as long as the flap and attach it to the corner of the flap. Push the flap inside the case, keeping the bead at the top of the opening so you can use it to pull the flap open.

Fun stuff

This chapter is full of fun things to make to decorate your knitted projects—knitted and felt flowers, chains, fringes, pompoms, and brooches. There are a few more simple projects to try once you've mastered the basic techniques. We even show you how to make a cushion insert, do some basic embroidery stitches, and use beads to add extra sparkle.

Chains, cords, and braids

Whether it's knitted, braided, or made in some other way, a cord is one of the most useful things to know how to make. Use cords for bag straps, ties, belt loops, belts, necklaces, and much more. Here are some easy ways to make chains and cords. And this is just the start—why not thread on some beads to jazz things up?

Simple braided cord

The simplest braid is made with three lengths of yarn. To make a thick braid, you can cut several strands of yarn and use them together to form one length. If you do use more than one strand, use the same number of strands for each of the three lengths, so that your braid is nice and even.

What you'll need
- Yarn
- Large safety pin

Here's how

1. Cut three lengths of yarn, or combine several strands in each of three lengths. Your finished braid will be shorter than the yarn you began with, so start with yarn that is about 2½–3 times longer than you want your braid to be. (If you want your braid to be 8 in (20 cm) long, cut your yarn lengths about 24 in (60 cm) long.)

2. Knot the three strands together and pin the knot to a cushion, or even secure the knot in a drawer.

3. Start the braid by moving the left-hand strand inwards and over the top of the middle strand. The strand you've just moved now becomes the middle strand.

4. Now move the right-hand strand inwards and over the top of the new middle strand. The strand you've just moved becomes the new middle strand. Keep moving the strands inwards in this way "left to middle, right to middle, left to middle," until the braid is as long as you want it.

5. When you have finished braiding, knot the ends together.

Tip
Before you knot the end of your braid, slip a bead onto the ends, then tie a knot—it looks really decorative and is a great idea for a belt.

Simple finger knitting

Here is a quick and easy way to make a simple, single chain from yarn. If you are left-handed, use your right-hand index finger to hold the loops of yarn.

What you'll need
- Yarn
- Your fingers

Here's how

1. Make a slipknot (see page 12) a short distance from the tail end of the yarn and slip the loop onto your index finger.

2. Holding the tail of the yarn under your other fingers, take the other end of the yarn over your finger in front of the slipknot loop.

3. Lift the slipknot loop up and over the front loop and allow it to drop off the front of your finger to make your first stitch.

4. Pull down gently on the tail of yarn to tighten the stitch.

5. Repeat steps 2 to 4 until your chain is the length that you want it.

6. To finish, break off the yarn, leaving a tail. Slip the loop from your finger, thread the tail of yarn through the loop and pull it up tight to fasten off.

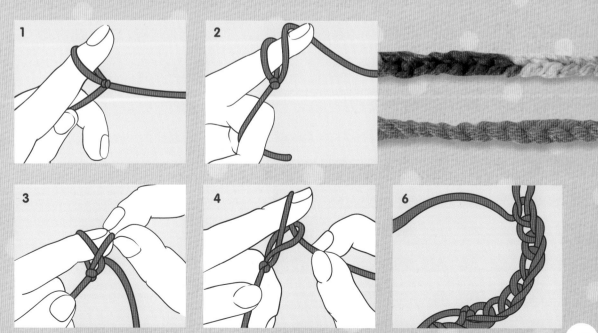

Knitted cord

This type of cord looks just like the one made from a little French knitting spool—sometimes called a Knitting Knobby—but it's much quicker and easier to make. You need to use a pair of double-pointed needles—they have points at both ends, so you can knit the stitches from each end. You can find them wherever you buy regular knitting needles.

What you'll need

• One pair of US 6 (4 mm) double-pointed needles

• DK weight yarn (or any other thickness)

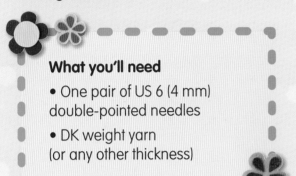

Here's how

1. Cast on 4 stitches on double-pointed needles.

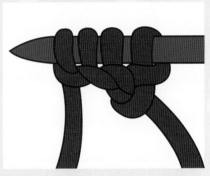

2. Work one row of knit stitch.

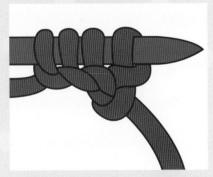

3. Instead of turning the needle around to start another row, push the stitches to the other end of the double-pointed needle. Your yarn will be at the "wrong" end of your work, but don't worry!

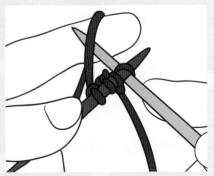

4. Simply pull the yarn tightly across the back of your work and knit the next row as normal.

5. Now push the stitches to the other end of the needle again, pull the yarn tightly across the back and knit another row.

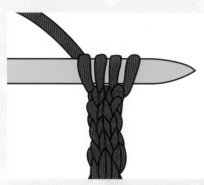

6. Keep knitting like this—pushing the stitches back and forth along the needle—until your cord is as long as you want. Pull gently on the cord as you knit, and it will magically close up into a tube!

7. Bind off.

Button loops and handles

Now that you've mastered the techniques, you can use your braids, chains, and cords to add button loops and handles to your funky bags, belts, and cushions.

Here's how

Sew each end of a short chain to the underneath of a flap to loop around a button on bags or cushions. Sew the ends of a longer chain along both edges of a bag to make a strap or handle.

Fringing

A fringe is a great way to finish off the edge of your knitting—whether it's a scarf, the edge of a skirt, or the flap of a bag. It's very quick and easy to do and looks really cool.

Basic fringe

What you'll need

- Yarn that is the same color, or a contrast color, to your project
- Scissors
- A medium-sized crochet hook

Here's how

1. Cut two pieces of yarn a bit more than twice as long as you want the finished fringe to be. Hold them together and fold them in half, so that you have a loop at one end and all four cut ends at the other end.

2. Push your crochet hook between the first two stitches of the bottom row of your knitting, from the back to the front.

3. Pop the loop of your folded strands of yarn over the hook. Pull the hook and loop slowly back through the knitting—but don't pull the yarn all the way through or you'll have to begin again!

4. Take the crochet hook out of the loop. Now, using your fingers, thread the four cut ends of yarn through the loop and pull them tightly. This will knot your first piece of the fringe in place.

5. Now repeat steps 1 to 4 along the edge of your knitting until you have completed your fringe. Clever you! The ends might be a bit uneven, so trim them to the same length with your scissors.

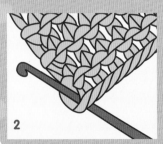

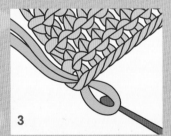

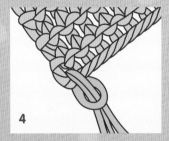

Beaded fringe

Add a few beads for that little extra sparkle to your fringe. Be sure to choose beads with a large enough hole to thread the yarn through—remember, some yarns can be quite thick.

What you'll need
- Yarn
- Scissors
- A medium-sized crochet hook

Here's how

1. Follow steps 1 to 5 of the basic fringe.

2. Using the strands of yarn from your fringing, just thread the beads onto the yarn and tie knots under the beads to secure them.

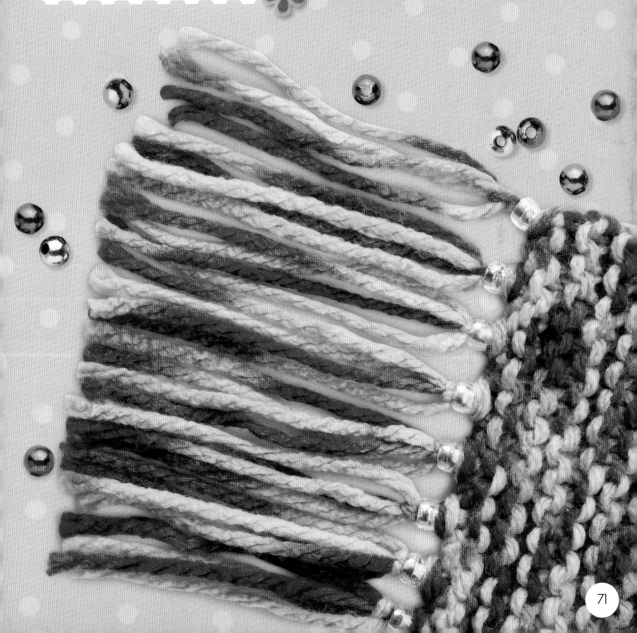

Pompoms

Pompoms can be any size, any color and in every type and thickness of yarn. The thinner the yarn, the fluffier the pompom. Add them to hats and scarves or make a whole lot and string them together as a very chic pompom scarf.

What you'll need

- Yarn
- Scissors
- Large, blunt-end needle
- Firm cardboard

Tip
Many craft stores sell little plastic pompom makers in a variety of sizes, which help you to make your pompoms very quickly. If you plan to make lots and lots of pompoms, a pompom maker might be the way to go!

Here's how

1. Trace and cut two cardboard circles. Your finished pompom will be a bit smaller than your cardboard circles. A good size to start with, while you get the hang of it, is a 3 in (8 cm) circle.

2. Cut straight into the middle of each circle and cut a small circle in the middle, about 1 in (2½ cm) in diameter. You should have two donut-shaped pieces of cardboard. Put both discs together.

3. Cut a long piece of yarn and wrap it around the discs, through the center hole. The more you overlap, the thicker your pompom will be. If you run out of yarn, cut more and keep winding. When it gets too hard to push the yarn through the hole, thread the end onto your large needle and keep threading until the hole is almost full.

4. Holding the discs in the middle, push the point of your scissors between the two pieces of cardboard. Keep your scissors between the cardboard circles and cut around the edge until you get back to the starting point.

5. Slide a piece of yarn between the two discs and wrap it tightly around the center. Pull it tight and tie securely.

6. Now carefully pull the pieces of cardboard out. Trim the pompom so it's nicely rounded, being careful not to trim off the long ties. Use them to attach the pompoms to your projects.

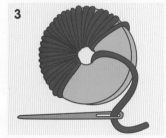

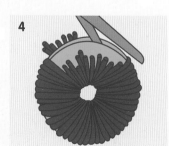

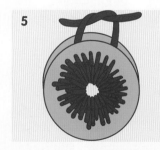

Knitted flowers

Knitted flowers look wonderful on hats, bags, cushions, headbands, and brooches. Here are a couple of different ways to make your flowers.

Circular knitted flower

These flowers make terrific brooches, especially with a pretty button in the center, or with two different size flowers on top of the other.

Measurements

These finished circles measure about 2¾ in (7 cm) in diameter

What you'll need

- DK weight yarn
- One pair of US 6 (4 mm) needles
- Large needle
- Button or felt circle

Here's how

1. Leaving a 4 in (10 cm) tail, loosely cast on 33 stitches.

2. Work 9 rows in knit stitch. (For a smaller circle, knit only 4 rows.)

3. Bind off, leaving a 4 in (10 cm) tail.

Finishing

1. Thread the tail of the bound-off edge onto your large needle and run it along the bound-off edge. Pull the tail as tightly as you can and secure with 2 stitches.

2. Weave in the thread on the wrong side of the circle. Thread the tail of the cast-on edge onto your large needle and join the seam by sewing through the side of the seam.

3. Secure with 2 stitches and weave the tail back along the seam. Complete your flower by stitching a button or felt circle to the center—or both!

Rolled knitted flower

This knitted flower looks a bit like a rose. It is very easy to make, but is best knitted on smaller needles than the standard US 10.5 (6.5 mm). A good size is US 6 (4 mm) needles, which was used to knit the flowers in the photograph.

What you'll need

- DK weight yarn
- One pair of US 6 (4 mm) needles
- Sewing thread and needle

Here's how

1. Cast on 30 stitches loosely on US 6 (4 mm) needles.

2. Work in knit stitch for 5 rows.

3. Bind off.

Finishing

1. Roll the rectangle strip around in a spiral to form a flower shape.

2. Secure the edges underneath with the ends of the yarn.

3. Layer smaller flowers for a great effect.

Flower brooch

Turn your knitted circles into neat brooches by decorating them and sewing a brooch pin or safety pin to the back.

What you'll need

- Knitted circles
- Buttons, lace, beads
- Circle of felt
- Brooch pin or safety pin
- Sewing thread and needle

Here's how

1. Decorate your knitted circles with buttons, laces, beads, felt, or anything else you would like.

2. Cut a circle of felt to fit one row inside the circle of the knitted flower.

3. Using your needle and thread, sew a safety pin securely to the center of the felt circle.

4. Sew the felt circle onto the back of the knitted circle. How easy is that!

> **Tip**
> Brooch pins are made especially for sewing to the back of your felt or knitted flowers. If you would rather use a brooch pin than a safety pin, you can buy them at craft stores.

Felt flowers

Felt flowers can be any size or shape, they look gorgeous on bags, hats, cushions, brooches, headbands, purses—just about anything! Follow these easy steps for a fancy flower.

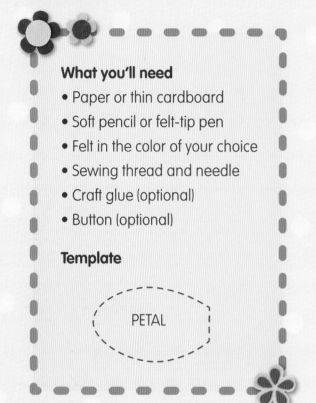

What you'll need

- Paper or thin cardboard
- Soft pencil or felt-tip pen
- Felt in the color of your choice
- Sewing thread and needle
- Craft glue (optional)
- Button (optional)

Template

PETAL

Here's how

1. Trace the petal opposite onto paper or thin cardboard and cut out to use as a template.

2. Trace around your template and cut six petals from your felt.

3. Arrange the petals so that they overlap and meet in the center. Sew them together in the center as shown.

4. Cover the center of your flower with a button or felt circle.

2

3

Tip
Instead of sewing the petals, you can also glue them to a small circle of felt at the back.

Making a cushion insert

If you knit a non-standard cushion cover, you might have to make your own cushion insert. You will need to cut two pieces of fabric that are ¾ in (2 cm) bigger than you want your final cushion to be. For instance, a 9½ in (24 cm) square cushion, requires two 10¼ in (26 cm) pieces of fabric.

What you'll need

- Enough plain cotton fabric or calico for the size you need
- Sewing thread and needle
- Pins
- Polyester stuffing
- Dried lavender or other sweet-smelling herb (optional)

Tip
If you can use a sewing machine, you can do this job much quicker!

Here's how

1. Cut two pieces of fabric, ¾ in (2 cm) larger than your finished cushion size.

2. Place the two pieces of fabric right sides together and pin the edges to hold them in place.

3. With a needle and thread, sew a seam around the edges, ⅜ in (1 cm) from the edge. Leave an opening about 4–5½ in (10–14 cm) on one side.

4. Clip across the corners with your scissors to remove the excess seam, taking care not to clip your stitching.

5. Turn the cushion cover inside out, poking the corners out neatly.

6. Fill the cushion fairly firmly with stuffing. Add a little lavender or other dried herb if you wish.

7. Fold in the edges of the opening and sew the opening closed. You're done!

Embroidery

Simple embroidery stitches can add the perfect finishing touches to your projects. Thread your needle, tie a knot in the end of the thread and follow these easy steps.

What you'll need
- Embroidery needle
- Embroidery thread
- Cotton, fabric, or knitted project

Running stitch

This is the simplest embroidery stitch and can be used in all sorts of ways. Although we call it an embroidery stitch when it is used decoratively, running stitch is also a basic sewing stitch, and can be used to sew things together and to gather edges when you want them pulled up tightly.

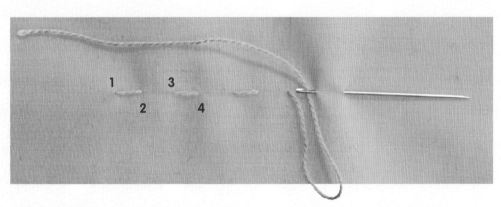

1. Bring the needle up from the back of your knitting to start.

2. Now put the needle back into the knitting a little way ahead of where it came out. The distance between these two points is the length of your stitch. Pull the thread all the way through to the back. You have made one stitch.

3. Bring it back to the front again, about the same distance from the first stitch as before, and pull the thread all the way through.

4. Take the needle through to the back again. Keep doing this until you have made a line of stitches.

Cross stitch

Cross stitch looks great on cushions and rugs. You make two single stitches in opposite directions on top of one another to make a diagonal cross.

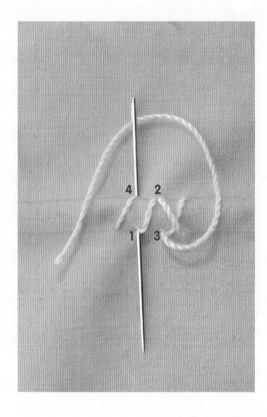

1. Bring the needle up from the back of your project where you want the first stitch to be and pull it gently through.

2. Put the needle back into the knitting diagonally opposite to where it came out.

3. Bring the thread to the front again, at the imaginary bottom right-hand corner.

4. Re-insert it at the imaginary top left-hand corner. You will see that you have now made a very real diagonal cross!

Tip
It helps if you imagine that you are sewing within a little square. If you imagine that the needle came out at the bottom left-hand corner of an imaginary square, you then insert it in the top right-hand corner.

Tip
Try to make all your stitches about the same length, as it looks nicer. This can be a bit tricky at first, but you will soon get used to it.

Easy Lazy Daisy stitch

Tip
You can sketch where you want your petals to be on the fabric then just sew over your sketch marks.

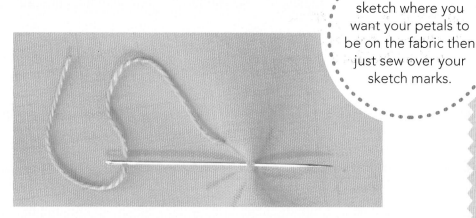

1. Bring the needle up from the back of your project at the outside edge of your flower. Pull it gently through until the knot stops it from coming any further. Push the needle back in near the center of your flower. This will be the length of your petal.

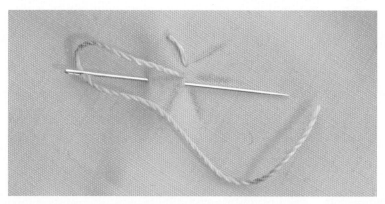

2. Pull the needle back up through the center of your flower a small distance away, to begin the second petal. Push it back through at the outer point of your second petal.

3. Repeat the simple stitches around a circle until your petals are complete.